dorkboy ∅ comics presents...

"WELL...THIS IS AWKWARD"

a collection of comics, paintings and junk
by damian willcox

dorkboy comics™ "WELL...THIS IS AWKWARD"
© damian willcox 2012
www.dorkboycomics.com

I0135936

introduction.

Many years ago during college, I had a brief stint with acrylic painting. Fueled by the thrills of working in a new medium and discount art supplies from the neighbouring art school's bookstore i was off and running in a world i knew nothing about. Acrylic paints were incredible – immediate, fast drying and much less nasty than their toxic older brother "oil paints". The stark, bold colours and consistency of acrylics also eschewed the wimpy demeanor of their other relative – the 'flowery' little sister, "watercolour paints" (which I understood was only to be used when creating artwork containing bowls of fruit resting on lace doilies in dilapidated rustic American cottages).

I created a number of paintings over the next couple of years using acrylics, until the mesmerizing world of comic creation drew me away with its much more accessible form of art and communication – where a painting might be seen by a handful of people, comics could be viewed, understood and appreciated by a much larger audience. I left acrylic painting, having never once tried oil painting and merely dabbled with watercolours in a night course that mostly reaffirmed my previous stereotypes regarding the use and subject matter of these paints.

For years in my comic creation work, I had used tools such as crowquill pen and ink followed by several years of nothing but digital pen and ink (as it didn't require the wrist pressure that traditional pen and ink had, which later manifested itself as tendinitis). In the last couple of years I have been sorely missing working with the traditional tools of the trade, but also mediums I had never given a successful or even fair attempt at. After more than a decade of comic making, I had never really grasped the classic linework tools of brush and ink. This was something I needed to tackle along with my severely limited exposure to watercolours. I looked everywhere for watercolour books and magazines in an effort to find inspiring works of art to motivate me – instead I found landscapes, fruit bowls and lace doilies.

I gave up looking for that book, and decided to make my own. This book contains a number of works I have made over the last couple of years, ranging in topics from robots to classic monsters and even includes one bowl of fruit for good measure.

I sincerely hope you enjoy it.

♥damian

Robotsロボット

As I collected my pieces of artwork for this book, distinct groupings began to emerge. Apparently I seem to have drawn more than a couple of robots along the way. This particular one will yield an optical illusion if you lay it down on a flat surface, as the robot will appear to 'pop' up. (don't worry he won't come to life)

"PLEASE RECHARGE"

"SPECIAL GUEST"

The dog in this picture is based off of our Jack Russell Terrier "Lychee". However, we do not own a robot like this... yet.

"THE DISCOVERY"

I always try to capture my paintings somewhere in the middle of a larger story that viewers are free to invent for themselves. And this is the sequel to that story.

"JUST BORROWING A CUP
OF SUGAR, NEIGHBOUR"

My best/worst neighbour. I expect it could go either way.

"LAST LUNCH IN THE PARK"

The person on the bench is me.
I rarely end up the hero for some reason.

damian 2012

"TIMIDBOT"

I should note that I have been very careful to ensure that most of the work in this book is actual size - so the robots on the adjacent page, as well as many of the other tiny watercolours in this book are actually that tiny in real life. You're picturing me making these tiny paintings with tiny brushes at a tiny desk now, aren't you? STOP IT!!

"HULABOT"

"GENTLEBOT"

"TRIUMPHBOT"

"RETROBOT"

"UNIVERSAL LANGUAGE"

one of two 'non watercolour' works in this book:
brush pen and copic marker from my sketchbook.

"LET IT GO"

Over the years I have been known to show fondness for the mail system. This has included mailing pieces of toast (unwrapped) around the globe, as well as decorating envelopes.

Shown above is an example of the latter. Name and address removed from the speech balloon for obvious reasons.

...and yes they do arrive at their destinations.

"LES ROBOTS TROIS"

Here is a collection of three tiny robot paintings I worked on in tandem, intended to be a 'set'.

(as opposed to the larger collection of robot paintings which is coincidence...or dumb luck)

"SCAREDBOT"

There may have been some 'Wizard of Oz' influence on this one.

"FRANKENSTEIN'S LAST BIRTHDAY"

Classic おばけ Monsters

2011 damian

"BRIDAL SHOWER"

I have always loved how iconic the classic "monsters" like Frankenstein, Dracula, the Wolfman and so on have become.

Naturally, they are the inspiration for these twists on the traditional classics.

The majority of these were created in a rather tiny format as you can see here.

"5 O'CLOCK SHADOW"

Someone get this man a razor.

"IT'S MORE OF A BLUE-GREEN LAGOON, REALLY"

"MUMMY"

"TINY DRACULA"

Don't be fooled – he may look cute, but he still drinks blood, just like those other monsters – mosquitoes.

"I'M SORRY, I DIDN'T SEE YOU THERE"

The Invisible Man has always been a favourite classic of mine.

"I LIKED IT BETTER WHEN I WAS JUST THE 'NOMINAL' SNOWMAN..."

There is a bit of a nod to Rankin & Bass' incredible work and beloved character the abominable snowman in here.

"CONTENTOSAURUS"

While not necessarily a 'classic monster' of sorts, this little dinosaur is what kicked off the monster paintings, and I would be remiss to not include him.

...also don't be fooled – he may be content, but he is surely a danger to humanity...look at him!

"THE PATCHWORK GHOST"

If you were to assume that I was a fan of **Tim Burton's** "Nightmare Before Christmas" from this you would be correct.

"GHOST OF A CHANCE"

This was one of my early watercolours as I began playing around
with "wet in wet" (painting on wet paper) techniques to get the
cloud like blue surrounding the ghost.

"FRANKLY SPEAKING"

This was done in a Rhodia
sketchbook with thin Vellum like
paper probably not intended for
watercolours...but did i listen?

"KING KONG LEARNS ABOUT EARTHQUAKE SAFETY"

Brush pen and grey Copic marker.
There is a chance I drew this in bed also....my
sketchbooks are everywhere

がいこつ

Skully.

damian 2011

"SKULLY"

One of my most well known comic characters is 'Skully' (pictured above) a naive yet lovable grim reaper.

Inevitably it seems, I have created a few Skully / skeleton based paintings in the recent past.

"SKULLY - SURPRISE VISITOR"

Here we have Skully and Skullkitty meeting a well dressed potential cohort to join their adventures.

Made with watercolour pencils which involves drawing with watercolour pencil crayons and going back over with a brush and water to magically turn it into watercolour....just like how milk magically turns into chocolate milk in your choc-o-bombs cereal. You get the picture.

I'm not even sure where to start explaining the backstory of this one. My wife, her mom and I were visiting Kobe, Japan where I stumbled upon an incredible little art store. I was left to my meager grasp of the Japanese language as my wife and her mom had gone on a few stores ahead. Despite my limited abilities, I was able to ask some questions about a Japanese watercolour brand called 'Holbein' I had yet to try. The folks at the store were incredibly kind and gave me a three colour (Red, Yellow Blue) sample of the Holbein paint. So on the slightly shaky train ride back from Kobe to Saitama, I inked the picture to the right with my Kuretake Brush pen and coloured it using only those three sample colours which seemed to be a big improvement from my current paints at the time.

damian 2012

"SKULL FLIP"

"BONE DADDY"

I've been a big fan of Miles Davis,
Ella Fitzgerald, and several other
jazz greats for years which inspired
this one... along with skeletons of
course.

12 tiny watercolours before christmas?

At various times, I have suddenly decided to challenge myself with self imposed contests of sorts – things like making a comic a day one February (that ended up a couple days short as I got a cold), and then in this case making 12 tiny watercolours exactly 12 days before Christmas knowing full well we were leaving for Japan early morning December 25 making it a very tight deadline.

"CANDYCANE LOVE"

"RAIN(COAT) DEER"

"FROSTY VS HOT CHOCOLATE"

I may have ruined fond childhood memories of yours with these next two. sorry.

"MILK AND COOKIES"

"I FEEL OVERDRESSED"

Surely I'm not the only one wondering why these guys are always naked? um, don't answer that.

"NOT A CREATURE WAS STIRRING..."

"NOT SO MERRY
CHRISTMAS"

I would like to think Santa
would never do this...

"TROUBLE IN
THE TREE"

"I FEEL LIKE I'M THROWING MY LIFE AWAY"

"SCROOGE IS VISITED BY MARLEY'S GHOST"

I imagine at this point "A Christmas Carol" would become a musical.

"REINDEER GAMES WERE ACTUALLY KIND OF GROSS"

Owning a dog has opened my eyes to all sorts of disgusting animal activity. Don't blame me for this one, blame the animals!

"BEING A CHESTNUT SUCKS"

Sadly, my last one came in a little bit late as I finished it a day or so after we arrived in Japan on December 26.

"GODZILLA VS MARTINI"

"VALENTINEZILLA"

Playing around with some paint
splattering on this one. Never
be afraid to get dirty.

"GODZILLA VS SHOELACES"

"GODZILLA VS MATH"

"WHICH WAY TO TOKYO?"

"FRIENDZILLA'S LAST VACATION"

It was merely a week or two after I created this that Japan was rocked with the disaster of March 2011. A real 'Friendzilla' was definitely needed.

Japan

Tokyo train platform

In March 2011, Japan was severely damaged by a combination of Tsunamis, Earthquakes and nuclear meltdown.

As my wife and I have family there, it intensified the horror and feelings of helplessness of watching the destruction from a distance.

Our family was safe, but numerous lives were lost and it serves as a strong reminder of how suddenly things can change in life, as well as the importance of appreciating loved ones while they are with you.

damian 2012

"SALARYMAN"

Two icons from Japan - the "salaryman" and the ubiquitous vending machines.

"GANBARE NIHON"

I created the painting above as part of an effort to offer my support and raise donations for Red Cross Japan.

"CHANGING TIDES"

This painting was themed with thoughts of rebuilding and recovery in Japan.

2012

damian

"YEAR OF THE DRAGON"

We brought in the New Year in 2012 in Japan, 'The Year of the Dragon'. Here's a drawing I made along with some photos I snapped on our travels.

まんが Comics

Many of the works in this book are more or less single panel cartoons, causing the line of when something becomes a comic and ceases to be a painting or illustration to become very blurry – so I tried to focus this chapter on multi panel comics to make things easier on both of us. You're welcome.

"THE EARLY WORM GETS THE BIRD"

"en plein air"

Friday Aug 19
2011
Galiano Island
B.C.

Galiano Island,
British Columbia

GALIANO AUG 20 2011 damian

This section contains some of my attempts at drawing outdoors ("en plein air") with my sketchbook, brushpen and watercolours.

This particular page includes sketches from a place called 'Galiano Island' on the Western edge of Canada. Imagine the setting for most of Stephen King's novels, and you have a pretty good idea of the place.

"LITTLE LIGHT"

This was drawn and painted at night in Universal Studios in Osaka, Japan while a parade complete with giant floats piloted by teacups and princesses singing "light up the night" marched by me just a few yards away.

At the same time, my wife and her mom were in a very long lineup waiting to ride the roller coaster I was too much of a baby to go on. In my defense I was still recovering from that scary 'Jaws' boat ride.

"CALGARY TOWER"

damian 2011

"COLD HANDS, WARM HEART"

I made this one from inside a coffee shop, and the one on the preceding page from a park bench near the tower as part of two different 'Sketchcrawls' where people from around the world go out sketching on a predefined day! For more information check out www.sketchcrawl.com

Fruits and 野菜と 果物 vegetables?

"A PAINTING ENTITLED 'OH GREAT, ANOTHER FRUITBOWL PAINTING' "

I'm so ashamed.

"WHEN BANANAS GO BAD..."

Drawn on a plane flying back to Canada from France. Of course, this has nothing to do with the image other than to say that inspiration and circumstance are rarely related.

"THE PICTURE OF DURIAN GRAY"

"THE PERILS OF BEING A TOMATO"

I have no idea how I ended up making so many personified foods – it wasn't intentional, honestly.

note to self: don't draw hungry.

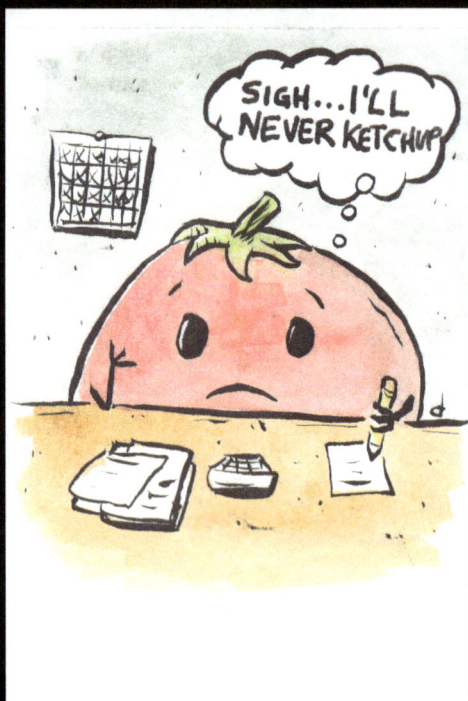

"OCTOBER 5, 2011"

In reference to a different apple.

"THE HUMAN BEAN, MISS EDNA WALKER AND THE AWKWARD PAUSE"

"THE PUMPERNICKEL ASSASSIN"

"SOMETIMES YOU CAN JUDGE A BOOK BY ITS COVER"

"ENTER THE CHOWDER"

Here we have my comic characters Kernel Corn and Peater the Black Eyed Pea testing the waters, so to speak.

The spirit of adventure!

The paintings in this final section thrive on action and adventure.

They will either leave you shaken or stirred.

"GAME OVER"

"MAJOR TOM'S LAST DISCOVERY"

"BATMAN AT THE LAUNDROMAT"

"I JUST REALIZED I'M AFRAID OF HEIGHTS"

"IRONICALLY, FLYING BANANAS ARE THE MAIN PREDATOR OF FLYING MONKEYS"

"FORBIDDEN LOVE"

Perhaps not quite aligned with the adventure genre, but surely bravery is involved in love?

damian

Fat Ninja has powers beyond any other
ninja, he also has some vices.

DRIP!!

damian

"FAT NINJA & THE STEALTH ICE CREAM RESCUE"

I ask you...if Fat Ninja doesn't rescue the
endangered Ice Creams of the world, who will?!

"CAUTION"

a spy? a secret agent?
either way she has firearms, so watch out!

"NEVERENDING HORIZON"

He is ecstatic that you have chosen to read his book, even though he had to write that in third person.

Thank you.

♡damian

www.dorkboycomics.com
damian@dorkboycomics.com

google+:   plus.dorkboycomics.com
tumblr: tumblr.dorkboycomics.com
twitter: twitter.dorkboycomics.com